Clock Wise Publishing

Winston Salem, NC 27107

For general information on our other products and services,

please contact us by email info@clockwisepublishing.com

Please like our Facebook page or follow us on Twitter for updates

 www.facebook.com/clockwisepublishing

https://twitter.com/ClockwisePublis

www.clockwisepublishing.com

Page Design by Ammar Elramsisy and Amanda Moss
Layout by Amanda Moss
Cover Design by Ammar Elramsisy

Recipe Index

Spice Blends

These spice blend recipes are referenced throughout the book, can be made ahead, and stored in an airtight container for easy access.

Salt Blend

1 cup iodized salt

½ cup garlic powder

Combine well and store in airtight container for up to 6 months

There are many Gluten Free blends available that are already prepared to save time. Emeril's Essence is listed as GF online. McCormick has many gluten free blends (Perfect Pinch, Gourmet) and all of their single ingredient spices are gluten free.

Spice Blend

8 Tbsp paprika

3 Tbsp cayenne

5 Tbsp ground black pepper

6 Tbsp garlic powder

3 Tbsp onion powder

¼ cup iodized salt

2½ Tbsp dried oregano

2½ Tbsp dried thyme

Combine well and store in airtight container for up to 3 months

Apple Glazed *Chicken*

Prep Time Approx **15** minutes

Cook Time Approx **35** minutes

1 lb thin boneless chicken breasts

½ **cup** apple butter

½ **cup** molasses

½ **tsp** salt blend (page 3)

½ **tsp** ground ginger

Preheat oven to 350 degrees and line rimmed baking pan with foil and rub lightly with olive oil.

In medium bowl mix apple butter, molasses, salt blend, and ginger until well blended.

Dip chicken in mixture and place on rimmed panned lined with lightly oiled foil. Spoon a little sauce on each breast to fill in bare spots. Bake for 25 minutes

Change oven to broil. Baste each breast with sauce and place chicken on top rack under broiler for 4 minutes.

Turn over chicken baste again with sauce and place on top rack under broiler for 4 minutes.

Serve and Enjoy

Bacon & Cheese
Drop Bisquits

Prep Time Approx 10 minutes

Cook Time Approx 12 minutes

½ **cup** sour cream

1 **Tbsp** water

1 **cup** gluten free baking mix

½ **cup** shredded cheddar cheese

¼ **cup** cooked/crumbled bacon

2 **Tbsp** melted butter

paprika

Preheat oven to 400 degrees

In medium bowl, mix sour cream and water until smooth. Add baking mix, cheese and bacon and stir until moistened. Drop rounded teaspoons onto a parchment lined baking sheet about 2 inches apart.

Bake approximately 12 minutes until the bottoms are golden brown and a toothpick comes out clean when stuck in the middle. Brush with butter and lightly sprinkle with paprika. Best served warm.

Variation: Pepperoni & Cheese Drop Bisquits - replace bacon with pepperoni and use mexican cheese instead of cheddar.

Notes: My preferred baking mix is Pamela's baking and pancake mix. If the tops are not browning turn the bisquits over and bake a few more minutes.

Serve Warm

Baked BBQ Chicken *Tenderloins*

Prep Time Approx 55 minutes

Cook Time Approx 25 minutes

½ **cup** brown sugar	½ **tsp** chili powder
1 **tsp** salt blend (page 3)	½ **tsp** paprika
2 **tsp** minced garlic	2 **tsp** BBQ sauce
1 **tsp** onion powder	½ **cup** BBQ sauce for basting

For the Marinade

Mix brown sugar, salt blend, minced garlic, onion powder, chili powder, paprika, 2 tsp BBQ sauce into a paste like mixture and brush on to lightly coat chicken tenderloins. Place basted chicken in gallon food storage bag and scrape the remaining marinade mixture into the bag. Seal the bag tightly and knead the mixture onto the chicken with your fingers. Place in fridge for 45 minutes to marinate.

For Basting - Preheat oven to 350 degrees

Pour 1/2 cup of BBQ sauce in a bowl and baste the chicken with a layer of bbq sauce. Once the chicken is in the oven, baste the chicken with bbq sauce every 5 minutes until done,

Cook for approximately 25 minutes or until the internal temperature reaches 165 degrees.

Serve and Enjoy

Baked Coconut Chicken

Prep Time Approx 15 minutes

Cook Time Approx 25 minutes

2 eggs

2 Tbsp milk

1 cup gluten free bread crumbs

¾ cup sweetened coconut flakes

2 Tbsp melted butter

1 lb thin chicken breasts

1 tsp salt blend (page 3)

Preheat oven to 375 degrees and line pan baking pan with parchment paper.

Whisk together the eggs and milk until well blended and smooth. In another bowl combine the bread crumbs, coconut flakes and melted butter with a fork until all the crumbs are moistened with the butter and the mixture is well blended.

Sprinkle the chicken with the salt blend, dip in the egg mixture and coat well. Press into the bread crumb mixture and roll over and press again until well coated and place in the pan. After doing this for each breast, Press any remaining bread crumb mixture onto any bare spots of the breasts.

Bake for 25 minutes or until the internal temperature reaches 165 degrees Serve with mango marinade, honey mustard, or any of your favorite sweet sauces.

Serve with Sauce

Baked Italian Green Beans

Prep Time Approx `5` minutes

Cook Time Approx `25` minutes

2 cans french style green beans drained and rinsed

2 Tbsp italian dressing or 1 Tbsp olive oil &1 Tbsp italian dressing mix (recipe below)

1 tsp salt blend (page 3)

1 tsp spice blend (page 3)

Preheat oven to 350 degrees and line rimmed pan baking pan with parchment paper.

Toss green beans in the baking dish with the dressing and spices. Stir well and cook for 25 minutes. Great to cook alongside your main dish.

Gluten Free Italian Dressing Mix

1½ tsp garlic powder	1 Tbsp onion powder
2 Tbsp ground dried oregano	1 Tbsp dried parsely flakes
1 tsp ground basil	½ tsp celery salt
1 tsp salt	1 tsp ground black pepper

Mix and blend well. Store in an airtight containers for up to 3 months.

Stir and Serve

Baked Pizza Spaghetti

Prep Time Approx 35 minutes

Cook Time Approx 20 minutes

12 oz gluten free pasta spirals

1 lb lean ground beef

1 cup finely chopped sweet onion

4 tsp minced garlic

½ Tbsp garlic powder

1 tsp dried basil

½ tsp oregano

½ tsp salt blend (page 3)

1 tsp spice blend (page 3)

⅛ cup freshly grated asiago cheese

½ tsp onion powder

½ tsp cumin

18 oz pasta sauce plus 1 cup

1 cup shredded mozzarella cheese

1 cup 4 cheese shredded mexican blend

3.5 oz pepperoni slices (approx 52 slices)

1 can sliced black olices (small can)

Preheat oven to 350 degrees and line 13x9 baking pan with foil and rub lightly with olive oil. Cook pasta according to instructions, drain and rinse with cold water. While pasta cooks, cook the ground beef, onions, minced garlic, garlic powder, basil, oregano, salt and spice blends, asiago cheese, onion powder, cumin until the beef is fully cooked. Add 18oz pasta sauce and simmer for 5 minutes.

For Layers - 1 cup meat mixture - 1/2 cup pasta sauce evenly on bottom. Spread 1/2 of the pasta evenly 1/2 of the meat sauce evenly- half the mozzarella and 4 cheeses evenly. Top with half of the pepperoni and half the black olives. Repeat and sprinkle lightly dry oregano. Bake uncovered for 20 minutes.

Broccoli Beans & *Rice*

Prep Time Approx 20 minutes

Cook Time Approx 10 minutes

2 cup diced onions

4 tsp minced garlic

1 Tbsp olive oil

1 cup uncooked white minute rice

1 ½ cup chicken broth

1 can black beans drained and rinsed

1 can red kidney beans drained and rinsed

½ tsp spice blend (page 3)

½ tsp salt blend (page 3)

1 tsp cumin

1 cup steamed broccoli

1 Tbsp gluten free soy sauce

Heat olive oil over medium high heat. Add onions and garlic. Cook for 3 minutes, stirring often. Add uncooked rice and stir constantly for 2 minutes. Add chicken broth, bring to a boil, cover and lower heat to medium. Cook for 2 minutes. Add beans, broccoli, soy sauce and spices. Mix well and simmer on low for 2-3 minutes.

This is a great healthy weeknight option. This dish can be paired with meats and vegetables, placed in a burrito, or just eaten with your favorite tortilla chips.

Quick and Easy

Caramelized Onion
Chicken Noodle Soup

Prep Time Approx 20 minutes

Cook Time Approx 35 minutes

2 Tbsp butter

2 med vidalia onions thinly sliced

8 cups chicken broth (2- 32oz cartons)

1 cup finely diced carrots

1 Tbsp spice blend (page 3)

½ Tbsp salt blend (page 3)

2 finely diced celery stalks

2 cups gluten free rotina pasta

2 cups cooked diced chicken

Melt butter on med low and add thinly sliced onion. Cook covered about 15 minutes, stirring occasionally. Turn heat to med high and uncover, stir constantly for about 5 minutes until nicely browned.

Heat broth, spices, onions, carrots, and celery over med high heat and bring to a boil. Stir in pasta and chicken. Separate with a pasta spoon for a few minutes. Reduce heat to medium and cook for 15-20 minutes until pasta is at the desired tenderness.

Special Notes: My preferred pasta brand is Tinkyada, this pasta doesn't clump and withstands longer cooking. Most importantly, Tinkyada doesn't have the taste and texture of gluten free pasta.

Homestyle Flavor

Chicken Fried Rice

Prep Time Approx 30 minutes

Cook Time Approx 10 minutes

- **1 lb** diced cooked chicken breast
- **6 cups** cooked sticky rice or white rice
- **1** sweet onion sliced 1" wide strips
- **1** large zucchini quartered and sliced
- **8 oz** fresh mushrooms sliced
- **12 oz** bag steamed petite carrots
- **3 Tbsp** butter
- **3 Tbsp** olive oil
- **6 Tbsp** gluten free soy sauce
- **3 tsp** salt blend (page 3)
- **2 tsp** spice blend (page 3)

Preheat wok to 300 degrees. Melt 2 tbsp olive oil and 2 tbsp butter. Add onion, steamed carrots, zucchini, and mushroom. Stir often with two wooden spoons to prevent sticking and cook for 3 minutes. Season veggies with 2 Tbsp of soy sauce, 2 tsp spice blend, and 2 tsp salt blend while cooking.

Add precooked sliced chicken, 1 tbsp olive oil, 1 tbsp butter and 2 tbsp soy sauce. Cook for 3 more minutes stirring often. Lower Wok to warm setting. Add the pre-cooked rice. Sprinkle rice with 2 tbsp soy sauce and 1 tsp salt blend. Stir constantly about 1-2 minutes or until internal temp reaches 165.

Japanese white sauce (shrimp sauce)   Whisk together 1 cup mayonaise, 3 Tbsp sugar, 3 Tbsp rice vinegar, 2 Tbsp melted butter, 3/4 tsp paprika, 3/8 tsp garlic powder. Chill for at least an hour.

Serve with White Sauce

Chicken Potpie
Muffins

Prep Time Approx 25 minutes

Cook Time Approx 18 minutes

2 cups gluten free baking/ pancake mix

½ cup butter or butter substitute

⅔ cup + 2 Tbsp milk

1 cooked chicked breast diced

12 oz gluten free cream of chicken soup

1 cup frozen mixed vegetables

1 cup shredded cheddar cheese

1 Tbsp spice blend (page 3)

1 tsp onion powder

1 tsp garlic salt

Preheat oven to 400 degrees and line muffin pans with cupcake 12 cupcake liners.

For Muffins - combine baking mix and butter with a fork or pastry blender and cut in the butter until the baking mix is crumbly. Add the milk and stir until a dough is formed. The dough will not be stiff. Pour evenly into the cupcake liners and create a well with a tablespoon in each muffin and press the muffin up the side of the liner.

For soup mixture -In a medium bowl, combine the chicken, cream of chicken soup straight from the carton/can, frozen vegetables, cheeses, and spices.

Fill each muffin well with the soup mixture, allowing the soup mixture to heap a little over the top of each muffin. Place muffin pans on top of a baking sheet and cook on bottom rack for 12 minutes. Move the muffins to the top rack and cook an additional 6 minutes or until the they do not appear doughy. Let stand a few minutes and serve.

Serve Warm

Corn Dog Muffins

Prep Time Approx 15 minutes

Cook Time Approx 24 minutes

½ **cup** melted butter ot butter substitute

6 eggs

4 **Tbsp** honey

½ **cup** super fine almond flour

4 **Tbsp** coconut flour

½ **tsp** baking soda

½ **tsp** salt

3 gluten free hot dogs cut into 1" pieces

½ **cup** shredded mexican cheese

Preheat oven to 325 degrees

Use a whisk to blend the melted butter, eggs, and honey until smooth.

Add the flours, salt, baking soda and cheese. Whisk more until smooth

Spoon 3 tbsp of mixture into each muffin cup or muffin pan slot (silicone muffin cups placed on a top of baking sheet work best)

Firmly put a hot dog slice in the center of each muffin cup.

Bake for approx. 24 minutes, I suggest turning the muffins 180 degrees halfway through cooking for a more even brown. Serve warm with honey mustard.

Serve with Honey Mustard

Creamy Skillet Rice

3 cups cooked white rice or sticky rice

2 Tbsp butter

½ cup finely diced red onion

2 tsp minced garlic

1 large tomato cut into ½" cubes (2 cups)

1½ tsp salt blend (page 3)

½ tsp spice blend (page 3)

½ cup GF ranch dressing

⅛ cup GF creamy italian dressing

½ tsp dillweed (optional)

Cook the rice according to directions

Melt butter over med high heat. Add minced garlic and onions, sauté for 2 minutes. Add tomatoes, season with 1 tsp salt blend and sauté for 2 minutes, stirring constantly.

Reduce to med low. Add rice, dillweed, spice blend, and 1/2 tsp salt blend. Cook for 1 minute, stirring constantly.

Lower to simmer and add dressings. Stir and simmer for 1 minute. Serve immediately.

Great Side Item

Cucumber *Salad*

Prep Time Approx 35 minutes

Cook Time Approx 0 minutes

2 english cucumbers

1 small red onion thinly sliced

1 can dark red kidney beans, rinsed and drained

1½ Tbsp course sea salt

2 Tbsp italian dressing

1 tsp sugar

1 tsp dill weed

Peel and quarter the cucumbers lengthwise. Then slice the long quarter slices into small 1/4" pieces.

Thinly slice the onion; Drain and rinse the kidney beans. Place the onions, cucumbers, and beans in an the over the sink colander or standard strainer. Toss with the salt and let sit and drain for 20 minutes. Gently press the liquid out of the vegetables and rinse well with cold water, the gently press a few times more.

In a medium bowl, combine the dressing, sugar, and dill weed. Stir well. Add the cucumber mixture and toss to coat evenly with the dressing and sugar mixture. Chill for several hours (at least two). Serve chilled.

Serve Chilled

French Dip *Sandwiches*

Prep Time Approx 15 minutes

Cook Time Approx 10 minutes

2 Tbsp butter

2 shallots chopped

½ Tbsp cornstarch

1½ cup beef broth

1 tsp worcestershire sauce

¼ tsp garlic powder

1½ lbs deli sliced roast beef

montreal steak seasoning

4 gluten free hamburger buns

Au Jus Sauce - Melt butter in large skillet over medium high heat. Add shallot and sauté for 2 minutes. Add corn starch to the butter and shallots; cook while stirring with whisk for one minute. Add the beef broth, worcestershire sauce, and garlic powder while whisking. Bring to a low boil and then lower to simmer to keep warm and thicken while preparing the sandwiches.

Sandwiches - Pile meat loosely on the cutting board and sprinkle each slice liberally with the Montreal steak seasoning. If desired spread a very light layer of mayonaise on the top of each bun. Grab several slices of meat with tongs and dip into the au jus sauce right before piling on the bottom bun. (be sure to let it drain a little by holding the meat up over the skillet for a few seconds before placing on the bun) Gluten free buns fall apart when soggy. So the idea is to have the flavor but not the sogginess. Repeat until the desired amount of meat is on each sandwich. I like to pile about 2 inches of meat minimum. Top with the top bun and serve with a small bowl of the au jus sauce for dipping.

Serve with Au Jus

Garlic BBQ Chicken
Pizza

Prep Time Approx `20` minutes

Cook Time Approx `25` minutes

1⅓ cup gluten free baking mix

¾ tsp dried basil

1 tsp oregano

½ cup bottled spring water

⅓ cup + 1 Tbsp extra virgin olive oil

2 eggs, beaten

5½ Tbsp honey bbq sauce

4 Tbsp pizza sauce

½ cup shredded mozzarella cheese

1½ cup cooken chicken (¼" cubes)

¼ cup finely chopped red onion

1 tsp minced garlic

¾ cup mexican blend shredded cheese

Preheat oven to 425 degrees
Cut flour with pastry blender or fork to remove the clumps. Stir in 1/2 tsp basil, 1/2 tsp oregano, bottled water, 1/3 cup olive oil and beaten eggs and mix until fully blended with no clumps of flour. Spread evenly with scraper or wooden spoon on pizza stone covered with parchment paper into a 12" diameter. Cook at 425 degrees for 15 minutes

Lower oven temp to 375 Once cooked remove from oven and brush with 1 tbsp olive until absorbed into crust and sprinkle with 1/4 tsp dried basil. Mix together bbq sauce and pizza sauce, spread evenly on crust leaving about 1" of the edges exposed. Sprinkle 1/2 cup mozzarella cheese evenly on top of the sauce. Lightly coat the chicken with 2 tbsp honey bbq sauce and evenly top on the pizza. Top the pizza evenly with the red onions and minced garlic. Cover the toppings with 3/4 cup four cheese Mexican blend. Sprinkle 1/2 tsp dried oregano on top and bake at 375 for 10 minutes. Cut with pizza cutter and Enjoy.

Slice and Enjoy

Greek Yogurt *Smoothies*

Prep Time Approx 10 minutes

Cook Time Approx 0 minutes

2 cups vanilla greek yogurt

1 cup orange or pineapple juice

2 Tbsp honey

16 oz frozen fruit smoothie blend

Place ingredients in belnder in same order as listed above and blend at pulse speed stirring occasionally until smooth.

Sip and Enjoy

Italian Chicken Strips over
Rotini Pasta

Prep Time Approx 20 minutes

Cook Time Approx 25 minutes

8 oz gluten free rotini pasta (I prefer Tinkyada)

¾ cup freshly grated asiago cheese

¾ cup gluten free italian bread crumbs

½ cup italian dressing

1 lb boneless chicken tenderloins

1 Tbsp olive oil

2½ cup marinara sauce

chopped parsely for garnish

Cook Rotini as directed on the package, be sure to stir with a pasta spoon occasionally to prevent clumping.

Mix together asiago cheese and bread crumbs in a small bowl. Pour dressing in a separate small bowl. Dip chicken strips in the dressing. Press chicken into the bread crumb mixture, turn and press again to coat evenly.

Heat marinara sauce on medium low and simmer covered while chicken is cooking.

Preheat oil in skillet over medium heat and cook chicken for approx 10 minutes, turning occasionally until the chicken is 165 degrees internally.

Serve sauce and chicken over the rotini pasta. Garnish with parsley if desired.

Garnish and Serve

Oven Fried Chicken

Prep Time Approx 20 minutes

Cook Time Approx 25 minutes

1 egg

2 Tbsp milk

2 cups crushed sour cream and onion or dill pickle chips (Lay's is gluten free)

24 oz chicken breast tenderloins

¼ cup melted butter

Preheat oven 350 degrees and line 13x9 rimmed baking dish with parchment paper

Oven Method - Crush chips in plastic storage bag. In a small bowl whisk together milk and egg. Dip chicken in egg mixture and then toss around in the bag and press into the chips one at a time. Place the chicken in a shallow baking dish. Drizzle melted butter over the chicken. Cook for 20-25 minutes until the internal temp reaches 170 degrees. Serve with honey mustard or your favorite chicken dipping sauce.

Air Fryer Method - This chicken is even better in the air fryer, just omit the melted butter and cook in two or three batches in the air fryer. Only place enough in the fryer to line the bottom of the pan for each batch and keep the batches warm on a cookie sheet in the oven at 200 degrees. Cook the chicken at 320 degrees Fahrenheit for approximately 15 minutes and you will have crunchy fabulous fried chicken without the grease.

Serve with Sauce

Potato Soup

Prep Time Approx 25 minutes

Cook Time Approx 30 minutes

5 lbs red potatoes, peeled and thinly sliced

32 oz chicken broth

1 Tbsp salt blend (page 3)

½ Tbsp spice blend (page 3)

2 cups half and half

½ cup butter

¼ white onion finely chopped

2 bunches green onions, finely chopped

2 celery ribs finely chopped

Combine potatoes and broth in a large stockpot. It is okay if the broth doesn't not fully submerge the potatoes. The potatoes only need to soften and more broth makes them too mushy. Bring to a boil. Reduce heat to medium and cook for 15 minutes until the potatoes are not mushy and very easy to break with a wooden spoon into smaller pieces. Gently cut into the potatoes with the wooden spoon creating bite size potato pieces. Season with the spices, pour in the half and half and mix well.

While the potatoes are cooking, melt the butter in large skillet over medium heat. Add the green onions, white onions, and celery. Sauté until the onions are translucent.

Add the onion mixture to the soup and stir well. Let simmer on medium low for about 10 minutes and serve. Garnished with shredded cheese.

Garnish with Cheese

Roasted Red Potatoes

Prep Time Approx 15 minutes

Cook Time Approx 45 minutes

2 lbs red potatoes cut into 1" chunks

¼ cup olive oil

2 Tbsp minced garlic

1 tsp salt

2 tsp spice blend (page 3)

Preheat oven 350 degrees

Toss potatoes with all the ingredients and cook in flat layer on a pizza pan or cookie sheet. (I line pans with parchment paper for easy cleanup and even baking)

Bake for 45 minutes stirring at least once halfway through cooking. Sprinkle with parsley and serve with your favorite dip or ketchup.

Sprinkle with Parsley

Rotini and *Meatballs*

Prep Time Approx `15` minutes

Cook Time Approx `35` minutes

1 lb lean ground beef	**¼ cup + 6 Tbsp** freshly grated asiago cheese
½ cup red onion finely diced	**1 tsp** spice blend (page 3)
1 tsp minced garlic	**1 tsp** salt blend (page 3)
1 Tbsp parsley	**½ tsp** cumin
1 tsp basil	**2 Tbsp** extra virgin olive oil
½ tsp oregano	**16 oz** gluten free rotini (I prefer Tinkyada)

Meatballs- Combine ground beef, onion, garlic, parsley, basil, oregano, ¼ cup asiago cheese, spice blend, salt blend, and cumin and mix well with hands. Roll meatballs into appox 2" balls (about 2 tbsp of meat) Makes approx 13 meatballs. Heat 2 tbsp extra virgin olive oil over medium heat and place meatballs in the pan. Cover and simmer for 3 minutes. Stir, turn each meatball over, cover and cook an additional 3 minutes. Drain meatballs and pour 32 oz of your favorite gluten free pasta sauce in the same pan. Simmer covered on med low while rotini cooks. I slosh the pan around every 4 minutes to prevent the meatballs from sticking.

Meanwhile heat water for rotini and once boiling add 16 oz bag of gluten free rotini , stir for the first minute constantly with a pasta separating spoon. Then every 3-4 minutes stir again to prevent clumping and sticking. I cook mine for 15 minutes. Drain pasta and rinse with cool water, gently shake colander to remove excess water. Pour the rotini into the pan with the sauce and meatballs. Stir well. Serve with the remaining freshly grated asiago cheese sprinkled over each serving.

Sprinkle with Cheese

Scrumptious Grill Cheese

Prep Time Approx 10 minutes

Cook Time Approx 8 minutes

8 slices gluten free bread

yellow mustard

8 slices thinly sliced tomato

8 slices of your favorite cheese (I use colby jack)

1 cup crumbled potato chips

8 slices crisp bacon

4 Tbsp shredded cheddar cheese

Spread mustard on one slice of each sandwich. Layer with cheese slice, two tomato slices, sprinkle on about 1 tbsp cheddar cheese, top with crumbled potato chips to cover equally, top with 2 slices of crisp bacon (I break them in two and crisscross), top with another slice of cheese and then with the remaining slice of bread. Squish down slightly.

Heat non stick skillet to med low or a flat griddle to 300 degrees, melt 1 tsp butter, cover and cook the sandwiches about 4 minutes on each side until golden brown. Watch closely to make sure they do not brown too quickly.

Serve with Chips

Sloppy Joes

Prep Time Approx 20 minutes

Cook Time Approx 35 minutes

- **1 lb** lean ground beef
- **½ cup** red onion finely chopped
- **1 tsp** minced garlic
- **½ tsp** salt blend (page 3)
- **1 cup** dark cola (regular or diet)
- **1 Tbsp** gluten free soy sauce

- **2 Tbsp** prepared yellow mustard
- **¼ cup** apple cider vinegar
- **⅓ cup** ketchup
- **2 Tbsp** sugar
- **1 Tbsp** gluten free worcestershire sauce

In a large skillet, cook the beef, onion, garlic, and salt blend over medium heat until the ground beef is brown and fully cooked. Drain the meat mixture. Whisk together the remaining ingredients and pour into the pan with the meat. Stir well and simmer to a low boil on medium. Lower heat to medium low and simmer until the sauce thickens, approx 25 minutes. Stirring occasionally.

Note: I am not a fan of red pepper, but you can add 1/2 cup of diced red pepper when cooking the onion and beef. Which will make it even closer to the original sloppy joe we all grew up with.

Serve with Fries

Slow Cooker
Cheeseburgers

Prep Time Approx 10 minutes

Cook Time Approx 190 minutes

1 lb ground beef	2 Tbsp spice blend (page 3)
¾ cup chopped onion	¼ cup ketchup
1 tsp minced garlic	1 Tbsp mustard
3 Tbsp ranch dressing dry mix	2 cups cheddar cheese

In skillet over medium heat cook ground beef, onions, minced garlic, spice blend, and ranch dressing mix until beef is cooked through.

Add ketchup and mustard, mix well and place in slow cooker. Pour the cheese on top and do not stir in.

Cook on low for 3 to 3 1/2 hours, stir well and serve on hamburgers buns. Top with your preferences, such as, tomato, lettuce, pickles. etc....

Serve on Buns

Slow Cooker
Chicken Tacos

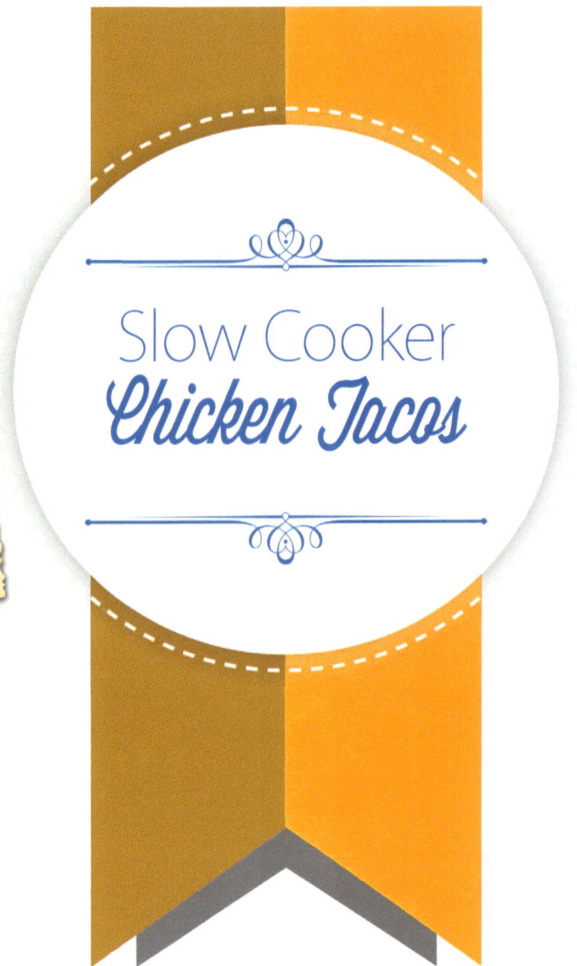

Prep Time Approx 10 minutes

Cook Time Approx 390 minutes

1 can black beans drained and rinsed

1 bag frozen corn

24 ounces chicken breasts

1 envelope gluten free taco seasoning

2 cups pico de gallo or chunky salsa

Pour black beans and corn in slow cooker and mix well. Place chicken on top of the vegetables and sprinkle lightly with salt blend or your favorite poultry seasoning. Pour entire envelope of taco seasoning on top of the chicken and then pour the salsa on top spreading lightly to cover all the chicken evenly. Cook on low for 5-1/2 hours. Gently pull the chicken apart with two forks. Place lid back on and continue to cook on low for another 30 minutes. Serve on your favorite gluten free tortillas, taco shells, or with tortilla chips. Top with chopped fresh onion, black olives, tomatoes, cheese, and sour cream.

Top and Enjoy

Slow Cooker *Chili*

Prep Time Approx `15` minutes

Cook Time Approx `420` minutes

1 lb ground beef	**½ tsp** dried oregano
2 cups chopped sweet onion	**¾ tsp** salt blend (page 3)
8 tsp minced garlic	**½ tsp** spice blend (page 3)
2 cans diced tomatoes (undrained)	**1 can** chili bean (bush bean's are best)
15 ounces tomato sauce	**1 can** kidney beans (rinsed/drained)
½ Tbsp chili powder	**1 cup** cooked white rice
1 tsp ground cumin	

Brown ground beef with the onions and garlic until fully cooked. Add all ingredients to the slow cooker, except the rice. Cover and cook for 6 1/2 hours on low. Add the cooked rice and continue to cook covered on low for another 30 minutes. Serve garnished with shredded cheese, a dollop of sour cream, and a side of corn chips.

Garnish and Serve

Slow Cooker
Vegetable Minestrone

Prep Time Approx 20 minutes

Cook Time Approx 480 minutes

4 cups vegetable broth

4 cups tomato juice

1 tsp salt blend (page 3)

1 tsp spice blend (page 3)

1 Tbsp dried basil leaves

8 ounces baby carrots coarsely chopped

2 stalks celery finely diced

1 cup diced onion

4 tsp minced garlic

1 cup mushroom finely chopped

2 cans petite diced tomatoes (14oz)

2 cups gluten free brown rice spirals

Place all ingredients, except the pasta, in the 4-6 quart slow cooker. The pasta will be added in the last 25 minutes. Cover and cook on low for 7 1/2 hours. Pour in the pasta (I use Tinkyada brand, which withstands heat very well and doesn't clump. Separate with a pasta spoon for several minutes, this prevents the spirals from sticking and clumping together. Set crockpot on high for 25 minutes. Serve and top with your favorite shredded cheese if desired.

Serve with Cheese

Sweet & Tangy
Cocktail Weinies

Prep Time Approx `15` minutes

Cook Time Approx `180` minutes

(2) **1 lb** packages gluten free hot dogs

1 cup brown sugar bbq sauce

1 cup concord grape jelly

½ tsp garlic powder

Slice hot dogs into 1/2 inch pieces (I use Nathan's brand). Mix together the bbq sauce, jelly, and garlic powder. Place hot dogs in slow cooker and pour the sauce over them. Mix well. Cook covered on low for 3 hours.

*These are always a crowd pleaser at parties and family get togethers , this is my grandma's recipe and has always been one of my favorites.

Serve Warm

Ultimate Ranch
Cheeseburgers

Prep Time Approx 15 minutes

Cook Time Approx 12 minutes

1 lb lean ground beef

3 Tbsp dry ranch dressing mix (1 oz hidden valley ranch packet is GF)

1 cup shredded mexican blend or cheddar cheese

2 Tbsp spice blend (page 3)

¼ cup gluten free bread crumbs

1 egg

Mix all ingredients together and form into four equal patties, put an 1/2" indent in the center of each patties for more even cooking. Sprinkle lightly with spice blend.

Preheat 1 cup of beef broth over medium heat until boiling and add beef patties. Cover with lid and cook for 5 minutes (do not open lid or press meat with spatula, this will allow the juices to escape.) Turn, recover with lid, and cook for an additional 4 minutes or until internal temperature is at least 165 degrees.

Remove from heat, sprinkle with cheese and let sit covered for 3-5 minutes. When serving let the juices drain a little before placing the patties on the bun to prevent the bun from getting soggy.

Alternate cooking method Preheat an air fryer 392 degrees F for 3 minutes and cook for 13 minutes or until the internal temp is at least 165 degrees. I can only fit 3 in mine at a time. so you may need to cook in batches if feeding more than 3 people.

Serve with Fries

Ultimate Teriyaki *Cheeseburgers*

Prep Time Approx 15 minutes

Cook Time Approx 12 minutes

1 lb lean ground beef

2 Tbsp gluten free teriyaki sauce

½ cup shredded cheddar cheese

2 tsp spice blend (page 3)

¼ cup gluten free bread crumbs

1 egg

¼ cup diced onions

Mix all ingredients together and form into four equal patties, put an 1/2" indent in the center of each patties for more even cooking. Sprinkle lightly with spice blend.

Preheat 1 cup of beef broth over medium heat until boiling and add beef pattles. Cover with lid and cook for 5 minutes (do not open lid or press meat with spatula, this will allow the juices to escape.) Turn, recover with lid, and cook for an additional 4 minutes or until internal temperature is at least 165 degrees.

Remove from heat, sprinkle with cheese and let sit covered for 3-5 minutes. When serving let the juices drain a little before placing the patties on the bun to prevent the bun from getting soggy.

Alternate cooking method Preheat an air fryer 392 degrees F for 3 minutes and cook for 13 minutes or until the internal temp is at least 165 degrees. I can only fit 3 in mine at a time. so you may need to cook in batches if feeding more than 3 people.

Serve and Enjoy

Weeknight Chili

Prep Time Approx 10 minutes

Cook Time Approx 20 minutes

1 Tbsp olive oil

1 lb ground chicken or turkey

1 cup sweet onion finely chopped

1 tsp minced garlic

½ **cup** pico de gallo or chunky salsa

1 can petite diced tomatoes (undrained)

2 cans chili beans (undrained)(bush's best is GF)

½ **tsp** chili powder

1½ **tsp** spice blend (page 3)

½ **tsp** salt blend (page 3)

1 can corn (I use green giant niblets)

½ **cup** celery finely diced

¾ **cup** mexican cheese blend

Add meat, chopped onion, garlic, spice blend, and salt blend, cook until meat thoroughly cooked and reached 165 degrees internal temp. No need to drain

Add salsa, celery, corn and cook about 3-4 minutes until tender crisp

Add tomatoes, beans, chili powder, 1 tsp spice blend. Bring to a boil and lower to med low. Simmer on med low for 10 minutes, stirring in the cheese in during the last few minutes.

Serve with Corn Chips

www.ingramcontent.com/pod-product-compliance
Lightning Source LLC
Chambersburg PA
CBHW042105040426
42448CB00002B/148